eMotion

Affirmative Poem
Part 2

Gloria Sarker

Dedicated to my Ancestors and Spirit Guides

ISBN 978-0-6454016-1-5
@Gloria Sarker, Melbourne, Australia 2022
eMotion-Affirmative Poem-Part 2

Contents

1. Today's Affirmation — 1
2. Queen Energy — 2
3. Appreciate Fear — 3
4. Abundance — 4
5. Fear — 5
6. What if — 6
7. Today's Journal — 7
8. Emotion — 8
9. Too much — 9
10. Auto-writing — 11
11. Anger — 12
12. Ready — 13
13. Let go — 17
14. I can do — 18
15. Funny Tummy — 19
16. Night shift — 20
17. Morning gratitude — 21
18. Looking for me — 22
19. My Focus — 23
20. Relax in a Crowd — 24
21. Holding back — 25
22. Feelings are ok — 26
23. Love and Wealth — 27
24. Inspiration — 28

25. Count my anger	31
26. My 3rd Eye	32
27. Procrastination	33
28. Emotional Wounds	34
29. My mouth	35
30. Generation	36
31. One Day	37
32. Dalilah and Deception	39
33. Bangladesh	41
34. My baba	42
35. My Mother	45
36. Complement and Confident	46
37. One Afternoon	48
38. In the bar	50
39. Self-Pity	51
40. Drop your dream	52
41. My feeling	53
42. Complain	54
43. My actions	55
44. Let it go	56
45. I can do	59
46. I know	60
47. I am	61
48. Rejection	62
49. Always find wrong	63
50. Beauty	64

1. Today's Affirmation

*I have the inner strength to face my fear
All fears come from inside
Nothing lives outside.
I listen to my higher self
I listen myself
My body and Spirit are friends.
I breathe with my soul.
I fear no more.*

2. Queen Energy

Queen is the opposite of the victim
Don't worry
I know I win
I own victory.
I have quality
I do maintain
That needs to keep
My wealth and prosperity
My purpose and strategy.
I am worthy
I love myself.
I feel
How it feels
Love and joy.

3. Appreciate Fear

*I find my inner strength
Peace and hope.
I know my anxiety and fear
They come out of nowhere.
I write my emotion
How they can be explained?
God gives me tools to learn
Fear and emotions.
This is my decision.
I am graduate
With gratitude
I find it good now
That was not good before.
I was blind
Now I can see
I grow in love
I know what is love
I know how to love.
I am love.
Thanks fear
You can stay near
I don't care.
You don't have power.*

4. Abundance

I live in abundance and hope
I know about the unknown.
I can see
Even if it's slow.
It's near and close.
I feel how it feels to receive
I allow myself
To receive
Bliss and gift.
I live in peace.

5. Fear

Where to go
Where to start
What to do

I know nothing
I keep walking
It is fun
It's a journey.

The dark days are past
Bright in ahead
I am kind and patience
I receive abundance.

Life is showing me its path
It has strength
Odds and evens.
Property, love, and victory.

My fear is my victory
I renew my minds
Live in joy each day.

I love myself
Seen and unseen
All beings
be happy
not survive
be thrive.

6. What if

What makes me fear
Failure, success, rejection
Illness or unknown.
Much to know.

What if a cyclone takes away all
What if I lose everything
What if I left alone
Rejected and loose
What if demons buy my soul
Darkness control me
Lost the light in life.
What if I lost the connection
With the source
What If I find myself alone?
Lost health and confusion.

What if I am angry and sad?
More guilt and shame
Lost hope
What if I am successful?

What if I am famous
Everyone knows
I am a billionaire.
I have love and life
I live in pleasure.
Purpose-driven life
Abundance and joy
It makes me flow of
balance and fulfilled.

7. Today's Journal

Today is a beautiful day
I appreciate the bird's chirping
My chicken's companionship
I love my house
My warn room
The comfort bed.

I love the big mirror on my bed
Warm heater in the cold morning
I love the peace in this place
The beauty all around me

I love myself
My wisdom
Courage
Kindness.

I love my enemies
People who hurt me
Love those who helped me
I say
Have a beautiful day.

8. Emotion

Feeling comfortable
Suppress emotion
Repress and slow down
All the pressure
Are anxious.
Focus on what I want
any other options?
Fire and water
Air and earth
All about balance.
Feeling comfortable
In uncomfortable
Go for fun.

9. Too much

*Everything is too much for me
The pending tasks, burdens
Undone jobs and overwhelm
All are too much.*

*Where to start
Let's do a journal
I am impotent
I want it now.
How far do I have to run
How long I can jump
Higher and higher
How far I can go
I feel I am left behind
I want my goal to be done.*

*Long way to go
I can wait and rest
The God does for me
My best is yet to come.
I need help
Includes validation.
How do I accept me
As it is.*

*Let my anger go away
Shame and sadness
Leave me now
Let me live in peace
Let go of my pride
Negative nights.*

*Let it balance
Let the energy stays*

What is next
Let it be settled
Curiosity and joy
No judgment
Stay behind
Rest and rejuvenate.

I am here for a big plan
I am blessed
Supported
Loved and
Let the joy and pleasure flow
Stays forever.

10. Auto-writing

Write down
I write down
All those upsets
I burn them
Blow the asses.

Revenge or Justice
Let my reborn life start
Let my unborn bloom
Manifest my womb.

Let me focus on my feeling
Express that makes sense
Pleasure and boundaries
Joy, peace, and compassion
Sad and frustration
Let me talk to them.

I have learned to express
All different
Same feeling
Name it

I am healed
I know how to express myself.
I have a beautiful life
That is balanced.

11. Anger

It was anger
I remember
My parents
I asked them
Many questions.

I want to know
Where do I belong?
Why have you done that or this?
I mean
All those mistakes
Parenting is a question.

My opinion of your decision
I don't accept
I was self-excluded.
I made my family journal
Never have any affection
Expression is complication
Love is hard
All about anger.

12. Ready

I am not ready
Not ready for love
I am learning
How to love
Perhaps self-love.

I am working on me
Myself
My worthiness
My healing
Balance
My intuition
Confidence
Self-esteem
My reality
And resentment
All blocks
That I repeat self-sabotage.

I am ready at that time
On the days
When I live in a unit
In a busy city
In my ensuite
I contact agents for tenants
for my houses
I rent the house of kindness
I have more space
For my office and studio
I publish books and youtube
I Start my business
Ready to purses the next houses
My business can go to all places
Then I am ready to meet you.
I can give you my stability

*Hope and quality.
It's not karmic
It is a legacy.
This is all I want.
I know you want to.*

*My gratitude to the universe
To give me my rewards.
I deserve better.
This time I am different
I changed
I grow and embrace.
I am attracting my best
You come to my door
With love and self-worth.
I learned how to live
with fun
Travel world
Act on Passion
We live forever.
Kindness and pleasure.*

13. Let go

Let go anxiety
Let go fear
Fear of lost
Fear of prosperity
Let go poverty
Negative self0talk and self-belief
I know I feel how it feels to be rich
To be wise
Wisdom and wealth.
Not anxious.

I let go of my past
Hurt
Vulnerable mind
I rather make my victory
Success story
I want to know
How it feels in wealth
Emotional balance
Body and mind rejuvenate.
How it feels to receive
Love that I deserve.
I forgive my past
Live in bless
Forgive me.

14. I can do

I can do more than this
I can do better than this
I don't give up
I keep doing
What I love to do.

I don't give up
I have answers
I have rewards.
I matter.

I walk through the mysterious
Wait and walk in the dark
Never give up.
It's hard.

Be patience
I can live my life in abundance
I can be happy
I am happy
I came from the dust
Return to the infinite dust
It is a must
I can do more
I can do better than this.

15. Funny Tummy

Funny feeling in my tummy
Can't tell my mummy
Funny tummy.

What makes it funny
Unsettled and frustrated
Worry and anxious
Mind and body
Restless.
I want accomplishments
Check my to-do list
No tasks have tick marks
I make my pain
I am impatience

I am harsh
Too hard myself
And it brings me hardship
It's my block.
I don't know rest
Relax and sleep.
I wake
and heighten.

Funny tummy
I am worry
It is bubbly
Who can help me?

16. Night shift

*Night shift
Way too long.
Long eight hours shift
All clients are sleep
I only awake
Doing my duties
Set tasks
More four hours
Night shifts.*

*Long many years
Night work
No routine
Only Day sleep
No comfort
My mind and body
Does not permit
No rest
Anymore
Tired always.*

*Night shift
New signs
Funny tummy
Sleep apnea
Snoring
teeth grinding
difficulty breathing.
Inflammation.
How long do to?
How many hours?
or years?
Makes me miserable
I am not kind.*

17. Morning gratitude

It's a beautiful morning
Thank you
Beautiful days ahead.
A day of joy and happiness
Day with fulfillment
A day of accomplishment
The beautiful sun shines
Lovely cold winter morning
The nice worm house
Heater
Blanket
Nice worm tea
Mice music
I appreciate
The life I belong to
I love the summer days
So do I appreciate the cold
Winter morning days.

18. Looking for me

Looking for me
Looking for love
I acknowledge you being there
I thank you to see me
I thank you for listening to me.

My dark past has been removed
My illusion is my vision.
I provide what I need
How do I serve me
For my best?
I hold all more tightly
I can do my work
I need to heal
I live the life that
I wanted
There is growth
Nothing can hold me back.

19. My Focus

*I focus on what I have
What I have achieved
I am nearly there
No one can stop.*

*I am living in abundance
I am healthy
I am loved
Loveable and worthy.*

*I have all that I want
I only ask.
I have family, friends, and wealth
Health and shelter
I have all that I want.
I give more to receive more.
I breath
I enjoy my days.*

*I enjoy my long walk
Cooking and gardening
I am progressing
Each day is a gift.
I am not worry
I focus on what I have
Not to what I don't have.
I am a gift
Each day is a gift.
I am living the life I dreamt of.*

20. Relax in a Crowd

I relax when I walk in a crowd
I am comfortable with the uncomfortable
I relax while I am moving
My heart is full of love
I enjoy my walk
In the crowd.

I am peaceful in the crowd
I act I focus
I am enjoying my change
I am enjoying my mess.
Each day is a blessing.

21. Holding back

I am holding back
My past
My lost love
My pride
My joy
My jealousy.

What is my learning?
What are my new paths?
What was right?
What was wrong?
What is next?

It's ok to hold back
I am enjoying my own time
There is a reason to receive a rejection
Refusal or disappointments
Show your strengths
Better days ahead
Better yet to come.
I am growing
No more holding.

22. Feelings are ok

It is ok to rise early or late
It is ok to sleep early or not
It is ok to feel sad or angry
Name it heartbreak or shame
Take some Nurofen.

It is ok to feel anxious or worry
All thoughts
Money or love
You deserve better
All are negative self-talk.
All are my thoughts.

23. Love and Wealth

*Love and wealth are coming to me
Each day I am getting closer to my prosperity
I am grateful to have all
That's all I want.
I am attracting
I am manifesting
My greatest desire
I serve
I received all.
I live in prosperity and happiness
I am grateful to have love and wealth.*

24. Inspiration

*Inspiration, creation
curiosity and encouragement
I can do
I am passionate to bring my dreams to true.*

*I am free
I don't live in poverty
It's a mentality.
Its misery
I am free.*

*I am happy to work
Purpose-driven life
Prosperous
Blessed
I am brave and confident
I love my life
I am love.*

25. Count my anger

I count my anger now on
1, 2,3
Each time I remember.

I remember all the unfair
disappointments
deprivation and frustration

I count what I don't have
more anger.
Distressed and disrespect
My low self-worth
It's hard to keep going
Let it go.

I am angry with myself and others
I seat down
I count my anger
1,2,3.

No actions.
I manifest anger more
I count 3, 4
more agro
fierce and aggressive
I learn
I grow.

26. My 3rd Eye

My 3rd eye is open
I feel the warmth
I know it was open always
I feel it
I listen.
I feel safe
I am protected.

My 3rd eyes are opened
I can see the past and future
It makes more power
I grow
I learn.
Each day
Each year.

27. Procrastination

My Ego is my story
My Mantra
My fear.
I don't care anymore.
No More.

I fear success
Fear of money.
Wealth and health?
They are not for me.

People will take away my money
Parents and siblings
Perhaps children
Particularly partner
All are my enemy
I love my money.

28. Emotional Wounds

I walk in confused
It was my wounds.
My life is messed
I am hurt
Not heard
Anger and resentment
Sad and violent.

My path is not straight
My thoughts are not enlightened
I work with mental illness
Hurting people hurt people
I work with merciful people.

My anger and hurts give me pain
Guilt and depression
I don't take any action.
I am addicted is my illusion
Illicit poisons.

29. My mouth

My mouth is the door of my soul
It can control me and you.
My mouth can cut you
Hurt you
Kill you.

My mouth can bury you
Leave you in misery
I am angry.
Sad and bitter
I have a long tongue.

My mouth is the door of my soul.
I can bring sweet, sour, or bitter
I can make it open or shut
That name is mouth.

30. Generation

*It's my emotion
Its rejection and abundant
Left me on the side
Low self-worth
It was my childhood.*

*My mother
Loved me so much.
I know now
You never expressed that much.
It was not kind.*

*I love you so much
You were not normal.
I am proud of you
I know so do you to me*

*I am the new one
Loving, kind, and gentle.
I change my beliefs
behavior and words.
I know you did try too.*

31. One Day

One day!
After long many days!
Yes!
One day!
We meet again.
We see each other again!
Seat in a quiet place.
One day!

I hope!
On that day,
We explain-
What has happened?
We tell each other-
What detached us?
We finally understand.
All questions will be answered.
One day we will be more mature.
For sure!
We will see how it did work for us.
We will see our past better.

One day we could not
return to our past.
Now at this moment,
I can rewrite my future.
On this day,
that will become my past days.

That future me
give thanks to my past days.
that helped me how to live?
How do love?

Until then I leave you behind.
Until then I live my life.
Until then I say goodbye.

One day you tell me
Why did you hide?
One day I realise,
why did I fight?
One day I know why did I cry?

One day we meet in peace.
Until then I let you go.
It meant not to be.
to be together!
Let me go. I wish you the best.
One day we talk about the details.

32. Dalilah and Deception

Samson said loudly last time
Almighty God!
Can you hear me?
Give my strength
My prayer is to Power back.

I am suffering from pain
They are mocking and entertaining.
Shame!

Please Return
my strength
I repent.

"Dalilah"
You are a beast
Beautiful and Evil,
Witch.

She was a liar and greedy
Foolish! I am!
I was blind.
Walked in deception
Lost in manipulation
She tests me many
for penny.
Why did I tell her?
My secrete
My secrets of power

I loved her
I trusted her
Witch!
I slept with my enemy.
Stupid!

Greedy evil!
Made a deal to kill.
Nagging many days
To know my secrete of strength.

I had time to leave her
Save my life.
Here who listens to my prayer
Leave them who betray the first time.

I made a devastating life
and should not trust the first time.
I am now blind!
In jail, waiting in the dark mist
Entertaining in the feast.

I pray loudly for my strength
Return!
I repent.

heart is pumping
do my last jumping
hold my arm in the walls
break in piece
kill them.
Middle in the feast.
My enemy Daliah!
It was my mistake
I went for a wrong street
Enemy and friends
Keep in faith.

Trust!
Before selling yourself
Love your people
fake or genuine
What remains
after the mistake
Only the pain.

33. Bangladesh

I came from light
As we all are!
I am light,
sending my love to them
who have nowhere to hide,
Only cry!

Shame Bangladesh!
Once more time!
How dare! You killed,
raped, and burnt those
who were supposed to enjoy the most?
During this Puja festival
I see smoke in the sky.
The red carpet of blood
Under the flowers of the rose!

I stand for my brothers'
shame on you Prime Minister!
Who will come after you?
when you done
Jongli Taliban?

I stand for light
I don't need to fight.
Peace on those
families and souls
who lost their lives
and valuables?

Bangladesh!
Where is your pride?
dark nights!
I don't fight.
I am light.

34. My baba

*Baba was 6 at 1946
worked in the crop field
daddy was with him.*

*Long wetland
only paddy rice green.
no island can be seen.
Little boat
Water
Quite in the early morning.*

*Deep dark mud
Leeches everywhere.
Sharp leaves and weeds
Sickle in hand!
Little child
used to cut the plants*

*Rest and harvest
after cleaning the leeches
from body parts.*

*Not knowing the time
Winter days no longer there
'Son, take a puff
of my cigarette
I have no bread'.*

*Comfort a little bit.
Papa was 6 in 1946.
Loved the puff of a cigge
until the lung stops breathing.*

35. My Mother

Dear Mother
I was confused
and you were too.
But we are together two.

I see all kids come out
to me it happens other.
You are my great-mother.

I know now
why you raised me
without a father.

I know now
why do you like to build the house
play with bikes
school and curriculum.

I know now
why you left the man behind
and love the rainbow color.

Now I know
why you write
to find the emotion behind it.

I love to hear
How did you feel
in the first time?
Is there any sadness
behind your happiness?

Mum we are together.
You gave me so much
Lots of love and care.
Let's watch Netflix
with Luca and a bowl of chips.

36. Complement and Confident

*Here are the complements
that make us confident.
Be authentic!
Good or bad
as who you are!
Whether have low-self esteem
Overthinking
pure in energy.*

*Left behind all
that don't need in the present
the new you are the best.*

*It's a reward
when we find each other
love arrives!
Triggers!
She Feels overwhelmed
with sleepless nights.
Fears!
Haunting past.*

*Move slow, relax
And take time
Let not the love cold
Let it flows.
There is a divine plan
Follow the flow
The path will show.
Its ok feel not good enough
Deep breath!
Tears drop on the papers
pen in hand.*

It is healing, youthful
Passionate and affectionate.
Cheeky chappy, creative
Charming, honest
Funny and playful.
It is within you.

Responsible and gorgeous
Blond hair and blue eyes
Mature, reliable
Independent and faithful.

Don't you dare give up.
It's ok if feelings are all over
Embrace the surprise meet up
Love is a gift that you deserve it.

It's ok to have possessive thoughts
It's not toxic or chaotic
but pure in peace.
Sexy human beings.

37. One Afternoon

You came to me
Stand nearby but
Not that near
I can call it near.

You touch slightly
It was not a touch
That I can call it a touch.

You seat next to me
Lean into me
But it was not close enough
That I can call it a lean proper.

You looked pretty and happy
Wear the bright dress
Cover with a little cardigan
Slightly shows
Your beautiful breast.

I wear a dress
cover with scarf
after the mess
in my linen cupboard
what to wear.
synchronicity everywhere
when love arrives.

I enjoyed you
Not enough
But good enough
That craves me to come to you later.

*You talked a lot
I felt you nervous
I was too.
I looked at you.
It was not a look
slightly stare.
I was alert in the crowd
to have a proper manner.
I pretended -
I was listening
to some words whispering.*

*I closed my eyes,
Blinked a lot
My tongue was heavy
Mouth was dry
I moved my neck
Right and left
Looked up and around
Deep breath!
I listen to your talk
that has no sense
I see,
You trying your best.*

38. In the bar

*You looked at me
Strange and weird.
I seat down on the bar
Did not have their drinks.
Gin or tonic.*

*I had my tea
That I carried with me.*

*I thought I should get up
Show some social manner
That I don't care.*

*I care you
I try to be friends
Who are with you?
I break my boundaries
Overwhelm!
Ordered some drinks
For your honoring.*

*You wanted to know me more
Softly asked me
"drugs or alcohol before?"
I seat down with my drink
That is called a non-alcoholic tonic.*

*Give me a little break
I need a deep breath!
The environment is toxic
I felt vomit.
I seat down
There was no place
to go and look around.
It is noisy and dark
All are blue
I can't see you properly.*

39. Self-Pity

*My mind plays
I think it's a game
I was pity
bitter and shitty.
Hello Kitty!
I was singing the song
"why me?"*

*It was not luck
I was fucked-up
hanging upside down.
I knew
I have to continue.
All my work
will make me empowered.*

*One day
there is reward
I shout
I am proud
in the crowd.
Hello!
I did serve.*

*It was not curse
not victim nor hurt
I have learned
I was loved.*

40. Drop your dream

I tell you drop your dream
I tell myself why?
I don't.
I love my dream.
My illusions are my dreams
I know my purpose
I stop myself to live in past
I live in the present
I live for future
I know my truth.

I better stop overthinking
It's like a matrix
I have a dream
It is real.

41. My feeling

*I want to feel first
before I get rich
I want to feel stable,
Happy and confident.
Before my love arrives.*

*I am feeling how it feels loved
I am feeling how it feels to be a wealth
I appreciate each day to be
loved, wealthy, and healthy.*

*It's in my Spirit
It's my feeling
It's my action
I am aware of more*

*I am learning more
I think
I act and
I feel.
This is how I get it.
I appreciate.*

42. Complain

*I make a list of
all my complaints*

*People mistreat me
Disrespect me
Judge me
Does not want to be my friend
People reject me
Refuse me
Use me
Takes advantage of me
People don't love me
People take my money
They are jealous
They control me
Abuse me
Misunderstand me
Put me down
Upset me
They don't care about me
They play with me
They don't support me
They manipulate me
They are not the friend*

*I make a mirror
I say all my complaints.
They echo to me.*

43. My actions

I open myself more
More polite
More humble.

I am open more to curious
More giving
More generous
More confident
More receiving
More asking.

I am more beautiful
More playful
More dreamer
And visionary.

I am opening my heart more
More calmer
More grounded
More down
More hope
More love

I am kind
Find more joy
More pleasure
More gratitude.

44. Let it go

Let it go
Let all hurts go
They are not welcome
Renewing my mind
Forgive and kind.

I change my patterns
My behavior
I change
I do my gratitude
I am worthy
I am valuable
I attract the higher vibration
Love follows.

I learned the flags
Green or red
Joy around me
All my wishes come true
Let me past
Stays in the past.
Let them go.

45. I can do

I can do this
I live in grace
Each different days
I live in faith.

My faith is my attitude
I am not running away
I learn
I grow
I develop.

I am in pain
I suffer
I know when it overcomes
My ego is angry
Frustrated and sad.

My ego knows its time close
Its roar will stop soon.
My spirit will bring me out
The real I am.
I am the co-creator.

46. I know

I know my next task
I know how to do that.

I am thinking
I am slow and silent.

I am preparing myself
The inner and higher self

It's my transition
In between the past and future.

I have learned my lesion
Success and protected
I was guided.

I know what I am doing
I have done this previously.

47. I am

I am mighty
I am great
I am lovely
I am brave.

I am smart and honest
I can trust
I listen
Be patient
creative
Curious
Humble
Polite
Impartial.

I am an influencer
I know my purpose
I help your goals.

48. Rejection

*Rejection is inside me
All feelings are killing me
When I feel rejection
I heard my childhood*

*Low confidence
Poverty
Fear
And low self-esteem.
I am no one
It was my trigger.*

*Rejection does not hurt me
Not anymore
My soul is at peace
No Destruction
No disappointments
I face all my fear
My rejections are
my redirections.
I follow my corrections.*

49. Always find wrong

I find the wrong people
It is my pride
I judge people.

I say myself
"stop"
Who am I to find wrong?

I am angry and negative
Low self-esteem.
All I can see
Critics others
Convict them.

My betterment
My resentment
I live in sorrow
Pain and guilt
Nothing melts
My heart keeps
Looking fault
It's my fight.
Who finds my faults?

50. Beauty

Beauty brings me a day
The Sunshine
No more rain
No cold
No wind.

I am enjoying the days
Long days I don't have great days
I am a magnet who flows
With fragments.

I have a new day
Another beautiful day
I feel better day by day
I feel my pain
Trapped emotions
I renew my mind.

www.ingramcontent.com/pod-product-compliance
Lightning Source LLC
Chambersburg PA
CBHW040243010526
44107CB00065B/2863